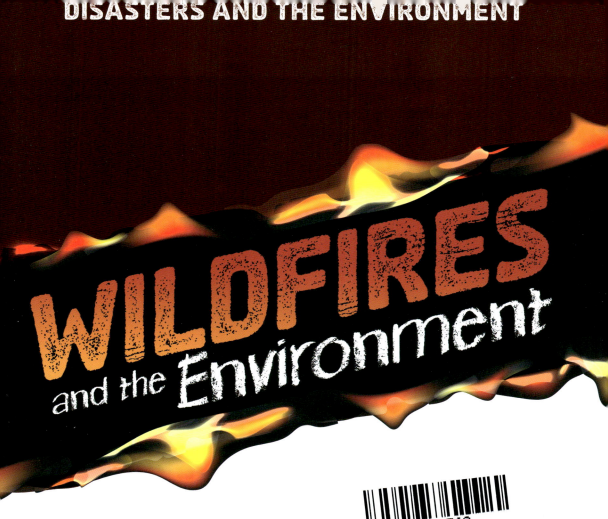

DISASTERS AND THE ENVIRONMENT

WILDFIRES
and the Environment

by Marcia Amidon Lusted

CAPSTONE PRESS
a capstone imprint

Published by Capstone Press, an imprint of Capstone
1710 Roe Crest Drive, North Mankato, Minnesota 56003
capstonepub.com

Copyright © 2025 by Capstone. All rights reserved. No part of this publication may be reproduced in whole or in part, or stored in a retrieval system, or transmitted in any form or by any means, electronic, mechanical, photocopying, recording, or otherwise, without written permission of the publisher.

Library of Congress Cataloging-in-Publication Data is available on the Library of Congress website.
ISBN: 9781669070924 (hardcover)
ISBN: 9781669071143 (paperback)
ISBN: 9781669071150 (ebook PDF)

Summary: Just one spark can cause a devastating wildfire. Entire neighborhoods can quickly be destroyed. Besides the impact on people, the environment suffers. Ash can pollute air and water sources. Animals can be killed or displaced. After a wildfire, soil can wash away and make it hard for plants to grow. Find out how people can help affected areas recover from a wildfire.

Editorial Credits
Editor: Carrie Sheely; Designer: Bobbie Nuytten; Media Researcher: Jo Miller; Production Specialist: Whitney Schaefer

Image Credits
Alamy: Design Pics Inc, 20 (right); Associated Press: Daily Inter Lake, Karen Nichols, 12, Jae C. Hong, 15 (bottom), San Francisco Chronicle/Gabrielle Lurie, 5; Getty Images: George Pachantouris, 23, Henrik_L, 20 (left), Justin Sullivan, 24–25, Kevin Trimmer, 6, Lucas Ninno, 9, Mint Images, 28, Mordolff, 29, RuudMorijn, 13, Scott Olson, 21; Shutterstock: Drop Zone Drone, Cover (bottom), Erik Agar, 19, Ethan Daniels, 26, Gchapel, 16, John Dowling, 11, LuismiCSS, 27 (bottom), Marcel Poncu, Cover (top), Morphius Film, 7, Nicole Patience, 15 (top), Nolichuckyjake, 27 (top), Orion Media Group, 17, Patricia Thomas, 18, Volodymyr Burdiak, 8

Design Elements
Shutterstock: Macrovector, PrasongTakham

Any additional websites and resources referenced in this book are not maintained, authorized, or sponsored by Capstone. All product and company names are trademarks™ or registered® trademarks of their respective holders.

TABLE OF CONTENTS

INTRODUCTION
Surrounded by Flames 4

CHAPTER ONE
Just One Spark 6

CHAPTER TWO
Changing the Land 10

CHAPTER THREE
What Happens to Animals? .. 14

CHAPTER FOUR
A Natural Recovery Pattern ... 18

CHAPTER FIVE
Humans and Wildfires........ 22

Glossary 30
Read More 31
Internet Sites 31
Index.................... 32
About the Author 32

Words in **bold** are in the glossary.

Introduction

SURROUNDED BY FLAMES

On November 8, 2018, a teacher drove to school in Paradise, California, and noticed that the sky looked orange. A wildfire had started when the wind blew down power lines. Dry pine needles, grass, and brush quickly caught fire. The wind grew stronger. The fire swept toward the town of Paradise very quickly. Fiery branches landed near children playing on their school playground. They had to get on a bus to get away from the fire. Soon everyone was told to **evacuate** the town.

FACT
The Camp Fire got its name from where it started near Camp Creek Road.

The fire came to be known as the Camp Fire. Causing 85 deaths, it was the deadliest wildfire in California's history. More than 18,000 homes, buildings, and other structures burned down. The towns of Paradise and Concow were nearly destroyed. The area burned covered more than 150,000 acres (60,700 hectares). In addition to the human impact, soil and water were **polluted**. Many animals died or were displaced. Scientists continue to study how the fire affected the **environment**.

People flee the Camp Fire in Paradise on November 8, 2018.

Chapter One

JUST ONE SPARK

About 70,000 wildfires occur in the United States every year. People cause about 80 percent of these fires. People can start wildfires by throwing away lit cigarettes or setting off fireworks. Campfires can create sparks that cause wildfires. Sometimes people even start fires on purpose. Natural events such as lightning can start wildfires too. Very dry conditions make it easier for fires to start. High winds can cause flames to spread quickly.

People need to be aware of an area's weather and surroundings before starting campfires.

In California, the area burned by wildfires has been increasing since 1950. Snow in the mountains has been melting earlier in the spring than usual. Temperatures in spring and summer have also been rising. This has caused drier conditions, which can lead to more and larger wildfires.

The Woolsey Fire burns in Malibu, California, in November 2018.

Wildfires can move very quickly. Some fires can travel 14 miles (23 kilometers) per hour. Fires that spread uphill move faster than fires that spread downhill. Fallen leaves and dry grass burn first. Then a fire can spread into the tops of trees. It burns from one tree to the next. Smoke gets thicker as the fire spreads to other areas.

Wildfires affect people, animals, and the environment. People who live in areas close to a fire may have to evacuate so they aren't injured or killed. Animals can tell when there is danger. Some can run away from a fire. But sick, old, or young animals may not be able to escape. Wildfires burn trees, shrubs, and other plants. Ash can pollute water sources and the air.

A hare flees a forest fire.

Case Study
2019 Bolivia Forest Fires

In 2019, wildfires in the country of Bolivia burned nearly 14.8 million acres (6 million hectares) of forest. Much of the destroyed area was protected land where a large variety of animals and plants lived. More than 2 million animals died, including anteaters, lizards, tapirs, ocelots, and pumas. Many jaguars live in the Pantanal. This wetland area is mainly in Brazil, but it also reaches into parts of Bolivia and Paraguay. Scientists estimate at least 500 jaguars were killed or left homeless in the fires.

Soon after the fires, Bolivia's government launched Plan Paradise. Through this plan, conservation experts will work with the military to restore plants in the Chiquitania area.

Wildlife in the Pantanal was greatly affected by the 2019 forest fires.

Chapter Two

CHANGING THE LAND

After a wildfire, the land is changed. Trees, shrubs, and other plants are burned. The ground is covered with ash, and burned tree trunks lie on the ground. The soil is no longer protected by plants, and it can't absorb rainfall. The soil washes away, and mudslides can flow into rivers and lakes. This mud can pollute rivers and streams. After a 2002 fire in Colorado, the South Platte River turned black with mud and ash that had flowed into it. Animals that drank from the river were poisoned.

The pollution of water sources can affect animals in other ways. It can decrease oxygen levels in rivers, killing fish. Changes in the levels of **nutrients** can also negatively affect aquatic life.

Ground Fires

Wildfires can burn in the ground itself. Tree roots and other materials underground can ignite and smolder for months. When conditions are right, they grow into bigger fires on the surface or in trees.

A wildfire can leave large sections of scorched land behind.

After a fire, a forest may be changed forever. Without trees and plants to hold rainwater, dirt can wash away. This washes the top layers of nutrients out of the soil. Plants need these nutrients to grow.

Small living things called **microbes** in soil help feed plants. These can be killed in wildfires. Scientists studied soil two years after Canadian wildfires. They found that the microbes in burned areas were very different from those in unburned areas. This may suggest that it takes a long time for soil to recover.

The Skyland Fire burns near Glacier National Park in Montana in 2007.

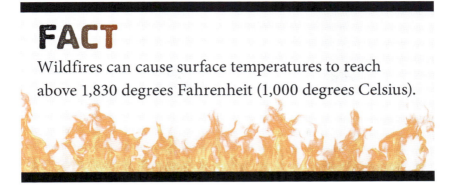

FACT

Wildfires can cause surface temperatures to reach above 1,830 degrees Fahrenheit (1,000 degrees Celsius).

Fire can also change what kinds of plants grow in a forest. After the wildfires in Glacier National Park in 2003, a plant called Tansy ragwort moved in. It crowded out native plants. After the fire, the park started a program to grow native plants and remove unwanted plants.

Tansy ragwort is poisonous to people and many animals.

Chapter Three

WHAT HAPPENS TO ANIMALS?

Animals have excellent senses. These can help them know when a wildfire is coming. Large animals such as deer and bears will run away. If they can't, they might stand in deep water. Fishers are members of the weasel family. They crawl into hollow trees for protection. Cottontail rabbits can hide deep in their **burrows**. Fish and frogs swim to the deepest water. If a fire is only a few feet high, birds and some other animals can go to treetops.

Some animals can't escape. Ash that flows into water can block the gills of fish and kill them. Large fires that move quickly and travel in treetops are hard for land animals to escape.

Feasts for Firehawks

In Australia, birds nicknamed "firehawks" fly above wildfires. They eat mice, lizards, and insects escaping from the flames. Some people say they have also seen the birds pick up flaming sticks and drop them into other areas. This is said to have caused new wildfires.

Fires can also ruin **habitats**. Animals then don't have the food and shelter they normally do. In the Sierra Nevada mountains, fishers and Sierra Nevada red foxes are **endangered**. Wildfires in California have destroyed much of their habitats.

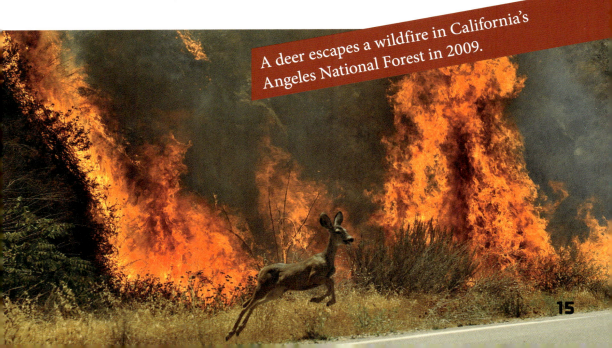

A deer escapes a wildfire in California's Angeles National Forest in 2009.

After habitat loss, small animals can have trouble finding food and shelter. **Predators** can then find them more easily. Birds that usually nest high in the tops of trees may not be able to find a place to nest or the material to make a nest.

Animals that survive wildfires may need to leave their habitats. Their habitats could be destroyed or changed too much for them to survive. By leaving, they may lose their shelter, food, or water sources. Water might be polluted by ash or mud.

Many animals return to the same breeding and nesting places each year. The population of an animal might take years to recover after missing just one breeding season. Sage grouse in Nevada have lost their nesting sites because of wildfires. They moved to other areas where their nests and eggs aren't as safe. There are now fewer chicks that survive.

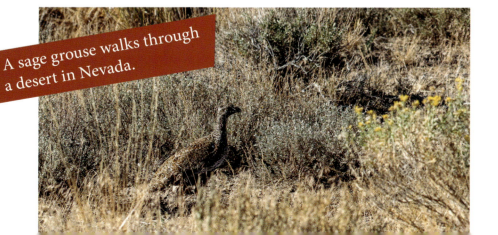

A sage grouse walks through a desert in Nevada.

Case Study
The Black Summer Bushfires

The Black Summer bushfires took place in Australia from July 2019 to March 2020. Lightning strikes started fires during hot, dry conditions. Billions of animals and insects were killed. Some were endangered **species** that may now be gone forever. After the fires, scientists were concerned about the populations of the Banksia montana mealybug, tiger quoll, mountain pygmy possum, carpenter bees, and other animals.

The International Fund for Animal Welfare and other conservation groups launched recovery efforts. Several endangered species have been helped by their work, including koalas, spotted-tail quolls, and red goshawks.

A veterinarian treats a koala that was injured in the 2019–2020 Australian bushfires.

Chapter Four

A NATURAL RECOVERY PATTERN

After a wildfire, plants begin to regrow. This happens in a natural pattern. The first plants to grow back in burned areas are flowers and weeds. They can grow from seeds that were buried in the soil and survived the fire. Grasses grow next. They grow well in burned areas because these areas typically have few trees. Shade is reduced and sunlight is abundant.

Flowers bloom around charred tree trunks in a forest burned by a wildfire.

FACT

The jack pine tree's pine cones hold seeds. The cones open after a very hot wildfire. New trees grow only when this happens.

Pioneer trees are the next to regrow. These are trees such as aspens, birches, poplars, and pines. They can grow even where the ground is bare. They can withstand high temperatures, full sun, and little moisture. When these fast-growing trees reach their full height, they create shade for trees that grow slowly. Their needles and leaves make the soil better for other plants and trees. Later, taller trees will grow.

Animals are also part of the pattern of regrowth. The first animals to come back are wood-boring insects. They eat the damaged trees. Some beetles even have heat sensors that find fire-damaged trees. Birds build nests in dead trees.

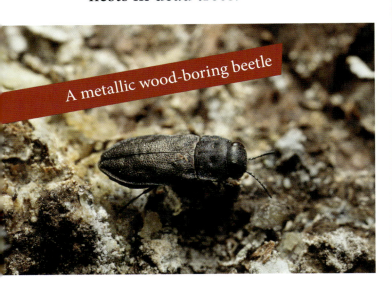

A metallic wood-boring beetle

A robin's nest in a burned-out tree trunk

FACT

Birds such as woodpeckers nest in dead trees and eat the insects found there. Burned trees from wildfires help the birds survive.

Soon chipmunks, mice, squirrels, and other small rodents return. Raccoons and foxes then come back. They eat the rodents and make burrows in the fallen trees. Finally, deer and other larger animals return. They eat the new green shoots of grasses and other plants.

Case Study
Fort McMurray Fire

The 2016 Fort McMurray fire in Canada swept through towns and forests. It burned about 1.5 million acres (607,000 hectares). Around 500 species of animals lost their habitats and were in danger from the fire. It also released poisonous chemicals into the air. They fell on soil and trees. Rainwater also washed them into streams and rivers. As part of a restoration project, more than 80,000 trees have been planted since 2016.

Smoke rises above the Fort McMurray fire.

Chapter Five

HUMANS AND WILDFIRES

Wildfires affect people in many ways. People can be trapped by the flames. They might be injured or die. Fires release large amounts of carbon monoxide and carbon dioxide gases into the air. People can have breathing and heart problems because of this air pollution. Drinking water can be polluted too.

Homes and other buildings can be damaged or destroyed. Structures built close to areas where wildfires happen often are most at risk. Roads can also be damaged. Communication systems may not work after a wildfire.

A wildfire burns in a residential area near Athens, Greece.

The way people make a living can also be affected. Crops may be ruined and farm animals can be killed. Trees used for lumber might be destroyed. People might need to find other jobs during recovery.

Wildfires can be very destructive. But they are also a way for nature to keep **ecosystems** healthy. They can create new habitats for animals. They can help add important nutrients back into the soil. The plants and dead material on the surface are burned. This makes some nutrients more available to the soil. Without a fire, it takes longer for the material to decay enough to release these nutrients.

Firefighters light a controlled fire in Glen Ellen, California, in 2017.

Smaller wildfires can help keep bigger fires from happening. They remove dry leaves, bushes, and fallen trees without burning the larger trees. Sometimes people start controlled burns. These small fires clean out dead material. They help new kinds of plants grow. Keeping any fires from happening is bad for the forest ecosystem.

Climate change has a role in wildfires. It creates drier, hotter conditions. These conditions lead to a longer time period during which fires are likeliest to occur and spread. This time of the year is called a fire season. High temperatures heat the air. This dries out soil and plants that are fuel for wildfires. Snowpacks on mountains shrink. This means less water for forests. Shifting patterns of rain and snow are also creating dry conditions in some areas.

Snowpack melts in the Sierra Nevada mountains each spring. It brings water to areas below.

FACT

Since 1944, the U.S. Forest Service has used the character Smokey Bear. The organization uses Smokey Bear to teach people how to avoid accidentally starting forest fires.

A huge smoke cloud rises over a wildfire in Spain.

Wildfires are an important part of the ecosystem. But extreme wildfires damage ecosystems and destroy communities. After many wildfires, it can take as long as 100 years for an ecosystem to fully recover. After severe fires, it can take much longer.

As new plants grow in burned areas, the ecosystem recovers.

How can people help? Some work to fight climate change. They might use solar energy in their homes. The sun helps create this kind of energy. People can build fewer homes close to wilderness areas. They might plant trees and flowers in areas affected by wildfires. Together, people can work to create healthy forest ecosystems and limit the damaging impacts of wildfires.

Volunteers plant pine seedlings in a forest that was burned by a wildfire.

Glossary

burrow (BUR-oh)—a tunnel or hole in the ground made or used by an animal

climate (KLY-muht)—the usual weather that occurs in a place

ecosystem (EE-koh-sis-tuhm)—a group of animals and plants that work together with their surroundings

endangered (in-DAYN-juhrd)—at risk of dying out

environment (in-VY-ruhn-muhnt)—the natural world of the land, water, and air

evacuate (i-VA-kyuh-wayt)—to leave an area during a time of danger

habitat (HAB-i-tat)—the natural place and conditions in which a plant or animal lives

microbe (MYE-krobe)—a living thing that is too small to see without a microscope

nutrient (NOO-tree-ent)—a substance needed by a living thing to stay healthy

pollute (puh-LOOT)—to make air, water, or earth dirty or harmful to people, animals, and plants

predator (PRED-uh-tur)—an animal that hunts other animals for food

species (SPEE-sheez)—a group of plants or animals that share common characteristics

Read More

Emminizer, Theresa. *Do Natural Disasters Change Ecosystems?* New York: Enslow Publishing, 2023.

Hubbard, Ben. *Wildfires and Freak Weather.* New York: Cavendish Square, 2024.

Jaycox, Jaclyn. *Wildfire, Inside the Inferno.* Capstone: North Mankato, MN, 2023.

Internet Sites

10 Wildfire Facts for Kids
wfca.com/articles/wildfire-facts-for-kid/

National Geographic: Wildfires
education.nationalgeographic.org/resource/wildfires/

PBS: Wildfire: Wildfire Basics
pbs.org/video/wildfire-basics-zfwzmx/

Index

animals, 5, 8, 9, 10, 13, 14, 15, 16, 17, 20, 21, 23, 24
  birds, 14, 15, 16, 17, 20
  fish, 10, 14
ash, 8, 10, 14, 16
Australia, 15, 17

Black Summer bushfires, 17
Bolivia, 9

Camp Fire, 4, 5
campfires, 6
controlled burns, 25

ecosystems, 24, 25, 28, 29

fire seasons, 26
Fort McMurray fire, 21

gases, 22

habitats, 15, 16, 21, 24

lightning, 6, 17

mountains, 7, 15, 26
mudslides, 10

nutrients, 10, 12, 24

Pantanal, 9

smoke, 8, 21, 27
Smokey Bear, 27

About the Author

Marcia Amidon Lusted has written 200 books and more than 600 magazine articles, all for young readers. She is the former editor of *AppleSeeds* magazine, and she also writes and edits for adults. Visit www.adventuresinnonfiction.com to learn more about her books.